# FEMINISM,

# IN OUR EVERYDAY LIVES

Dress yourself down

Don't be too pretty if you're smart

Watch what you're saying

# The Modern Feminist Adovcate

# INTRODUCTION

*Why am I writing this book anonymously? Because I know that once my employers discover how strongly passionate I am about feminism, and read this book, they will reconsider me as an employee. That's what our world is like in today.*

I find it very inspiring that our female ancestors have fought for our freedom and rights. After all, how could we have otherwise been able to go to school today, vote, be protected from rape, sexual harassment at work, in schools, and work in relatively powerful positions? I am so thankful that I was born as a millennial because I'm so privileged to have been born _into_ these readily available rights. I did not know any other way of life. So firstly, let's say thank you in acknowledgment to those who have fought for us, who went to jail for us, who were hit for us. Let's be grateful for those who were willingly tortured for future generations, ourselves.

I am personally very happy that feminists have successfully fought for those major milestones. At least legally, we have "privileges" now.

That being said, that does not completely radicate the sexist mindsets of people today, especially those of the older generation who unfortunately are still in control of the workforce. I am so thankful obviously for female-owned companies. However, not everybody is entrepreneurial, and unfortunately still today, the majority of companies providing jobs to societies are mainly male owned. Why does this distinction matter? Simply because when someone is in power, they set and impose their own rules on others. Generally, those rules are not considerate of females' perspectives or needs. Us women have very different and particular needs that men could not even foresee. Generally men in power view women their own ways, through their own filter, and hold them accountable to standards that they themselves impose on someone that is different than them.

As I was going into the workforce after graduation, it felt like I was going into battlefields. Why? Because I felt like I needed to debunk stereotypical myths about me every single day that negatively affected my supervisors' impressions of me. Every single day, I consciously tried to not look too pretty, minimize my makeup, not wear colorful nail polish, keep my nails short enough to remain unnoticed although I loved the art of nail extensions, not overly smile an act as professional as I could. Although I was little confused because I did not know what that embodied. How can I become something other than myself? Who even decided anyway that smiling was unprofessional? I needed to consciously avoid naturally smiling which I usually do a lot since I am a happy person, to ensure that my supervisors were not thinking that I was flirting with them or interested in them in any romantic way. It was very constraining, it felt like prison. It was so difficult for me to adopt a personae that was not authentic. I had to do it though because I knew that I couldn't change my employers. They gave me jobs, it was thanks to them that I was training my career skills and feeding myself. Don't we all think about this? How much perfume we use? How we do our hair? How we stand or walk to "look" as professional as possible to those in power?

As a millennial, I always questioned why it was even considered unprofessional not to smile, *especially* for attractive women. I feel like we are being held at a much stricter standard because it can very quickly be interpreted that we are flirting. How is this our fault? Why is it that looking attractive makes some appear less smart, competent or professional? Rather, for *me,* the question is, why do I need to come *into* a space where those in power do not know me at all, and start by proving that I am not the negative stereotype commonly thought of? Why is it automatically presumed as a premise that I'm the negative stereotype to start with, anyway? It all seemed to me very backwards. Do we hold these same assumptions about men? I strongly doubt it considering the edge they have in the workforce. I remember how baffled I was when I looked at EVERY *single* national and international law firm's demographics and found out that 75% of the owners were men. Almost 90% of managing partners were men, which means that they decide where the business goes, and administer finances etc. I felt sick for going into a boy's club. "Great" I thought, "Now I have to live under their standards, and they will be controlling me 24/7". That was not pleasant at all. They had all the cards. Most importantly, I couldn't help but deeply question the frustrating and mysterious fact that on the employee level, the amount of female and male lawyers was equal. It was only on the ownership and management level that it became drastically disproportionate, favoring men. My head started spinning. It was the same pattern at every law firm. It was very difficult for me to narrow my job search to female owned firms because they weren't the majority.

I think this matters on so many levels. First of all, as an associate, I usually work long hours for my superiors and many of those times, they call me into their offices after-hours, to "discuss" issues. It makes me very uncomfortable to risk escalations this way. It's a vulnerable position I fear being in. Second of all, I need to try to put myself in men's heads and try to dress in a way that would maintain their respect for me. I want to obviously maintain their serious impression of me so they can appreciate the quality of my work in an unbiased way. It's a very difficult situation to be in, because now I not only should consider what my heart and artistic sense wants me to wear, but also the negative impression it will make on some other gender that I cannot fully understand. So I have two hurdles to overcome. I don't really understand why I have to be in this position in the first place. Just for being a woman? HOW IS IT MY FAULT THAT I WAS BORN A FEMALE? What is so wrong about wanting to be artistic and colorful with your clothes? This is what theorists call the female guilt: being guilty for just being female. Feeling guilty about having boobs by trying to hide them as much as possible, avoiding talking about them, or "trying" to make them look decently respectful, feeling guilty for our vaginas, for our soft voices (many of us) that are rarely taken seriously, and for our general way of being.

"That's just law", you may say. My female consulting friends work in business consulting firms that are also owned by men. To fit into the work culture, they have to watch baseball, hockey and basketball games "to build a bond" with other male employees and clients. It is very reasonable to bond with someone based on their interests. But when does the scale tip over onto to the female side? Aren't others interested in our hobbies and interests? It makes us feel invisible. Not to mention the very obvious awkward way men in the corporate world communicate with women in a belittling and disrespectful way. We shrug it off because this is our livelihood, it is how we make our money. However, those everyday struggles are battles we face everyday that silently tell us "we don't have power", "we are invisible", "we don't matter" because we are not the ones running the show. The business show at least, which generates money thus freedom and power. How can women feel comfortable and become free from those stereotypes and indirect sources of control? If making good money in the corporate world won't cut it, we are only left with starting our own companies.

Those issues are not covered by legal rights or anything formal. They are very subtle and are raised in the details of our surrounding's interactions with us on a daily basis. I cannot stress enough the importance of our subconscious mind's potential of controlling our lives. Usually the subconscious mind absorbs information and core beliefs through repetitive actions or reactions. If you repeat a message enough times to it, it will ultimately internalize it and believe it. Then, your subconscious mind ends up making you behave a certain way to comply with those beliefs, because you are not in control of your subconscious mind; it controls you, believe it or not. There is expansive research and study on this topic. We cannot accept the reinforcement of subtle yet incrementally loud sexism in our daily lives. Not every woman is an entrepreneur, and some institutions, such as universities, don't easily open the gates to female professors. What options are left in that case? How do we stay away from everday sexism, yet focus on our goals to succeed and have an impact on this world?

# QUESTION EVERYTHING

One very important lesson I took away from my feminist legal courses is that if you think that the world simply is the way it is for no reason, you're wrong. The world is the way it is because the people in power built it a certain way and maintained this structure, still today. You can observe it in the way old men talk to women, the way your outfit is judged no matter what professional position you have (referencing commentaries in the media about Michelle Obama and Amal Clooney's clothes and makeup while they were advocating for very serious causes), the way you're treated while having sex, while being sexual or courted, the way men respond to you in your everyday life and, the criteria under which your candidacy is evaluated as you enter university or apply for jobs.

Everything revolves around culture. I don't mean countries' particular cultures. I mean the culture under which a person is raised from a very young age. I mean the way in which you were loved by your mother or father, how you were treated at home, in school, by your friends, teachers or colleagues. What did all these experiences teach the men in question? No reaction or action comes from thin air. Everything derives from a source, especially human interactions, they derive from a cultural source. Even if you consider establishments such as schools, churches, governments, companies, partnerships, hospitals etc., they were ALL designed by someone, under certain standards that people had. Now, those were unfortunately established by men and they do not necessarily meet all our human needs. Why? Because originally they were not designed *by* women and *for* women. They were designed *by* men *FOR* men, first and foremost. When an institution or establishment was designed for women, it was designed to put females in a box that men believed women should be in. They created activities and institutions for them to develop those skills that men believed should imperatively master. Men kept relegating and confining women to the private and domestic spheres that the public spheres became dominated with men, and that's where the major and critical developments were made and **built** for a man's world.

Now you may say that things are changing and women are going into the workforce and even dominating it. Surely I agree. What I urge you not to forget however is that women are *ENTERING* into an already existent and established system. They are not *CREATING* it from scratch. Uprooting is a challenge that every human resists. Uprooting an entire system is not an idea that will be gladly welcomed at least considering how the dominant ones within the most powerful forces like the academic world and the working field are *STILL* men.

Question why dark suits are considered appropriate, elegant and professional and not other type of wear. Consider why heals are viewed as professional and sometimes unprofessional by others. Consider why you force yourself to act in a certain phony and fake way to attract respect. We are living in a world that unfortunately believes that seriousness, exceptional talent and competency are correlated with the color of clothes you wear, lack of smiling, lack of kindness, and fake confidence. Who even stated that confidence is key to success? It is only this way because men foolishly buy fake confidence. Confidence never helped me succeed my courses or become the powerful person I am today. On the contrary, it was rather the lack of confidence that helped me succeed. Thanks to my lack of confidence, I doubted the thoughts, theories and beliefs imposed on me. I questioned twice what I was thinking, believing, saying and learning, which helped me verify my work thus made it excellent, and developed in me a very strong critical analytical thinker. When I was blindly confident on the other hand, I overlooked details believing "I'm good enough" and slacked off. In my eyes, the simple fact that you need to pretend to be someone else to succeed in today's world, is the only proof I need to conclude that our world is not built under sustainable foundations that will increase our happiness and human fulfillment in life. Success and productivity from my experience are the fruits of a happy, comfortable and authentic person. Why else would people say follow your passion? Because passion, comes from your heart. It comes from a place that you naturally care about developing. You do not need to pretend you're good at it, because you are too busy authentically caring about mastering it and learning more about it. The fact, by the way, that the word "passion", according to my employing mentors, is taboo in the work force, drove me further into disagreement with this world's present construct. Who made this this way?

*MEN*

# DON'T FALL INTO THE TRAP OF EXISTING SYSTEMS

When I grew up, I was listening to my role models speak on Youtube and on television. I chose to be raised by them, voluntarily, as a child. I read their books and bought their merchandise. I followed their advice religiously to the letter. Their general mantra was to promote authenticity, lack of identification with our egos, and following our passions and curiosity, because it was going to lead us to success and happiness in life. Going into the workforce however, it seemed like the predominant philosophy was completely opposite to the one I grew up listening to and applying. I couldn't understand how two very opposing mindsets could coexist in such dominant ways. It was when I graduated, and while I started looking for my first "real" job, that I noticed the difference between self-made entrepreneurs and the established corporate world.

The former promote freedom, spirituality, belief in one's potential, authenticity, hard work, second chances and the love for mistakes. The latter promotes conventionality, fitting in rather than standing out, fake confidence, political (or "schmoozing") skills, and the concealment of your unusual talents and interests. Self-made entrepreneurs promoted following your curiosity no matter where it lead you because your learned skills were certainly going to aid you as you go into your next venture. The corporate world however promoted sticking to what you already know based on where you came from and "logical" transitions into more specialized fields. The corporate world didn't judge you based on your skills that are sometimes immeasurable, it judged you based on the quality and reputation of the institutions you attended and the organizations you joined and contributed to. It was all about fake image and fake confidence, I concluded. Little does the corporate world know, that I learned much more in non-famous organizations than I learned in famous and reputable organizations. Interesting, isn't it?

If you do not want to be traditional, and fit into this traditional world view, I suggest you follow a path to financial freedom, but also a path where you will be able to be authentic, in public, as a woman. I used to believe that change can happen once you infiltrate the system. I use to believe that you can change a system from within, but clearly this has not been working because women have infiltrated the system for a considerable amount of time now. I would say about two generations worth of time. What I suggest now, is to counter attack from the side, having used a different vehicle to your freedom as a woman. If you are comfortable with the corporate world, all the power to you. However, I see it as very challenging to shake the boat and change things from within.

On the other side, I think that building your own company and business would favor your comfort and autonomy which could lead to your confidence and sense of security when promoting a different way of life as a woman. For example, if you question for example the system of a company while you're an employee or even a co-owner, you can easily be cut off from that source of income by being fired or, disliked and later fired. However, if you already established your independent source of income, the stakes are much lower when it comes to risking your source of income. You would thus find it more encouraging to promote change because people will believe in you and when people believe in you, it is always easier to monetize that power of influence in today's world. With our technology today, we are more equipped than ever to make that change. As a woman, it couldn't matter less what your interests and passions are because you can find a way to monetize them thanks to today's technology. From thereon, growing your financial portfolio will only require getting skilled at and learning more about scaling your business, branching out, marketing, and diversifying your services or products. Not to mention financial skills. I learned that money doesn't discriminate between men and women, because if you go down to the roots, money is an element exchanged between any two people for acquiring value from the other person. Value, can be anything. Everybody _needs_ **something.** It doesn't matter what it is. So you can fill that gap, while still remaining true to yourself and acquire assets from it. Instead of going into already established institutions that have been built centuries ago and trying to fit into that and ultimately believing that that is the way of life, **make your own institution** and make THAT the way of life that you would like to see in this world, as a woman!

# YOU DESERVE TO DEFINE THE WORLD AS YOU PLEASE AND TO IMPOSE YOUR WORLDVIEW

I will never forget what my legal feminist course taught me: that the major way men disadvantaged women was to diminish and steal their voices. The remaining consequences of this action are still present today. One concept that absolutely blew my mind was that men previously felt entitled to talk about and even define things that **did not** belong to them or were not related to them, in an objective way. They felt objective and neutral enough to talk about and define women according to their filter yet portray their opinions as an objective view. You can even notice it when you pay close attention to how they define things or explain things in our everyday life. Many, I noticed, explain concepts and talk about women like they know who we are, what we like, how we think and what we think when we act in certain ways. They talk about the world like they know what it is, they interpret it "objectively" yet according to *them.* They completely filter daily situations their own ways and pretend that their view is THE objective view. When it came to women, our views, according to them, are deemed subjective and biased, which discredited the legitimacy of our opinions, desires and worldview. As a result, it is their worldview that humans end up relying on, as the neutral perspective and default guide. We do that without paying attention because we never questioned them when they said things like "that's the way the world works". No, that is not the way the world works, it's the way you forced it to work, now I want it to work *my* way, which should equally be THE way.

I remember the old texts my professor brought into our seminars demonstrating to us how the main historical authors, not so long ago, were predominantly men. The misfortune is that our history is biased by men defining everything through their own filter yet "objectively". Consequently, we only know the history from their point of view. We only know the milestones that they care about. Not the ones that affected us, women, or affected our own interests. I suggest for us to be mindful of such ongoing behavior nowadays that may subtly lean towards this historical pattern mentionned above. Being aware of it helps us stop it in its tracks, and control what feeds our subconscious minds everyday.

# INTERNALIZATIONS ARE REAL

It was thanks to my legal feminist courses that I dug deep into internalizations. I learned that, as explained above, our subconscious mind internalizes many beliefs based on everyday interactions, actions and reactions. Many are much more subtle than you imagine and expect them to be. For example, what do I think of a woman who is very sexually active or overtly sexual? Say, Kim Kardashian for example in her photoshoot. What do I really think of that? Once you ask yourself deep questions and get brutally honest with yourself about your feelings towards certain acts or events, your internalizations come up.

Personally, feminism for me, means the ability for a woman to do whatever she wants, yet still be respected regardless. So for example, if Kim Kardashian wants to show her bottom in a Magazine shoot, does that mean I should respect her less? Why would I respect less a person who is showing their body? If it was a man, would my feelings be less intense? I think most people would be less shocked by a man showing his bum in public. Just because someone is comfortable about revealing their bodies does not make them mentally less capable or deserving of respect and admiration. That is my main definition. Feminism, in my view, does not necessarily mean cutting your hair short, not wearing nail polish or being aggressive. It could 100% be that if that is what you define it! I support your view of feminism. But why should there be one imposing and rigid view of what certain women believe other women should be? We are going against the freedom we originally fought her. Why don't we just give each other the freedom and social respect for being whoever we want, dress however we like without being judged and act however we like?

I interpreted our historical feminist achievements as ones whose main focus was to bring freedom to women. Freedom brings happiness and fulfillment. Freedom, to me, means being able to be who you want, dress how you like, talk as you wish, think as you please, and still be able to have the potential for the greatest success and respect, regardless of how outside of the norm it may be. What I even advocate for, is to have a premise of respect when we see behavior that is outside of the norm, regardless of how successful or non-successful that woman may be. The tables can turnover very fast, unexpectedly. We should support each other, as women, to do whatever we want and appear however we like, without fearing attracting danger to us because of that.

# HOW WE CAN APPLY THIS TO INTERSECTIONALITY

This leads me to my last chapter about intersectionality.

Intersectional sexism means that yes, many women only face discrimination based on their gender, being female. Nevertheless, so many other women face discrimination on many more factors such as racism, age, socio-economic status and more that add up. Sexism, combined with those other factors upon which discrimination may be based, creates a very unique experience of sexism that these women face. For example, women who are part of a minority, are already almost invisible in the eyes of society, unfortunately. If you add to that the problems that sexism raise, it doubles the prejudicial effect on these women. They face a very certain type of discrimination that none of us can truly understand, except for the people in those positions. So when we train ourselves to accept what is out of the norm, I believe this will also have a positive effect on us as women by training and preparing us to give a voice to and respect the experiences of those who face so many different discriminations that we didn't care enough to listen or understand. When we, as women, reinforce the feeling of invisibility of other women, we are not contributing to making them feel respected.

Being respected means being heard and having your voice impact the world to an extent  that it at least changes things in your favor. In order for us to fully contribute to feminist changes in the world, we must give every opportunity to every woman out there to express herself and respect her for it. Because no woman is free until all of us are free, by empowering each and every one of our voices.

What do you think?


Do you agree or disagree?

We would love to start a conversation about this, to get more women involved in feminism, spread the word, and support each other.

If you enjoyed reading this essay, please feel free to write a feedback on Amazon.com.

1. Type "Amazon.com" in you website browser

2. Type "Feminism: in our everyday lives" into the search box.

3. Click on the book, and let us know at the bottom of the page what you think in the reviews.

We would love to spread the word about feminism, and educate as many women as possible.

Help us share this essay!